I0486729

EIGHTSTORM

8-Step Brainstorming
for Innovative Managers

EIGHTSTORM

Kishore Dharmarajan

Copyright © Kishore Dharmarajan

All rights reserved. No part of this publication may be reproduced,
stored in a retrieval system, or transmitted, in any form or by any
means, electronic, mechanical, photocopying, recording or
otherwise, without the prior permission of the publishers.

Published by Book Surge LLC, an Amazon.com Company.

Eight tools that will have you bursting with innovative ideas in your next brainstorming session.

Contents

Introduction

I believe that in the future there will only be two kinds of businesses: Businesses that innovate and those that do not. When they compete in the marketplace, it's quite obvious which of the two will survive and thrive.

In fact, history is full of these unbalanced encounters. The Railways killed off the Stage Coaches. Telephone finished off the Telegraph. Mobiles wiped out Pagers. And in recent times the iPod has done away with the Portable Cassette Player.

Once we accept the fact that business cannot live without innovation, the next question is how does a business become innovative? How can we come up with an idea that could be the next big thing in the market? How can ordinary mortals like you and me become thinking geniuses?

Let's read Eightstorm and find out.

Kishore Dharmarajan

EIGHTSTORM

THE BOSS WAS DEAD.

He was found in a hotel room with a bottle of forbidden pills scattered on the floor.

It was hard for Joe to believe that the President of the company was dead. This was the man who had turned the company from a simple outfit in a sleepy town into a vast organisation with operations in several countries.

Why had the boss committed such a callous act? Why hadn't Joe seen it coming, especially as he was so close to the President? He had no problems with his family, thought Joe as he left the hotel room, wiping the sweat off his brow. *Why had he done this?*

The next couple of days were a tumultuous affair for Joe like the other employees, as the company desperately tried to steady itself after the loss of its President.

They sat with charts. They analysed. They drew up plans. They discussed till the coffee turned cold. And slowly, the company came to terms with the nasty reality: it was sinking. What was even more shocking was the fact that the downfall was brought about by the very person who had built it - The President.

Was this why he had committed suicide?, wondered Joe, as he sat in the uncomfortable meeting room.

For years the company was riding its fortune on a single line of products that was the market leader in its category. And now suddenly, without any warning, a competitor had come up with an alternative that made their line outdated. In the space of a few weeks cancelled orders were piling up in their warehouses.

Something has to be done quickly, Joe thought as he drove home late that night. *Someone has to come up with a breakthrough idea that can save the company and bring back the lost glory.*

Joe's train of thoughts was interrupted when his mobile rang. It was Vitae, his childhood friend, who was now with an extremely dynamic company in another part of the country. He had heard of the President's death and the problems in Joe's company.

'We've been through a similar situation,' Vitae told Joe, 'but we managed to pull through. We had a person on board who brought in Eightstorm.'

'What was that?' Joe asked.

'Eightstorm. It's a new kind of brainstorming process,' Vitae explained. 'Instead of bouncing off ideas against one another, we used...'

The line wasn't very clear. Vitae's voice trailed off and the mobile line got cut.

Hello, Helllooo, Helllloooo, Can you hear me?... Joe yelled into his mobile, but there was no answer. He tried to call Vitae back, only to hear an automated voice telling him the number was unreachable.

I need to meet Vitae, Joe thought, *and if it means flying out tonight, I am going to do that.*

Instead of driving home, he headed towards the nearest airport.

The night flight was delayed by fog, so Joe took a good four hours to reach Vitae's city and another 30 minutes in a cab to reach his office.

'What a surprise!' Vitae exclaimed, seeing a tired-looking but grinning Joe in the reception room of Vitae's office. 'So you took a quick flight to see me, eh!'

'I had no choice,' Joe answered.

'Let's go to my cabin, it's around the corner.'

'Look, I know what a mess your company is in,' Vitae began after they had settled down in Vitae's cabin, 'and you know as much as I do why it went down. I see more and more companies like yours making the same mistakes, and it makes me sad.'

Vitae seemed lost in thought for some time. 'I don't want to give you a long-winding lecture on what you should've done to avoid this circumstance or how to get your company back into shape. Instead I suggest you see what we are up to here.'

'You mentioned something like Eightstorm

over the phone. What is it?' asked Joe.

Just as he was going to answer the question, Vitae's mobile rang and he picked it up.

Vitae was on the phone for some time and Joe got bored sitting on the sofa for long.

As he got up to stretch his legs, Joe noticed a crystal cube on Vitae's table. He walked towards the table to take a closer look. There was more than one crystal cube on the table.

Joe picked up the first cube which had 'I' etched on it. It felt smooth and cold.

By now, Vitae had finished his conversation on the mobile and joined Joe beside the table.

'This is what Eightstorm is all about,' Vitae proclaimed. 'You have been asking me what Eightstorm is all about. Here it is. The entire session on a table.'

'Don't look at me like that,' Vitae said laughing at Joe's puzzled face. 'These are the cubes that we use in our Eightstorming sessions. Each cube you see is a tool. For example you are holding the Interrogate tool in your hand.'

'I for Interrogate. That's interesting,' said Joe. 'What does N stand for?'

'N is for Navigate. You see our Eightstorming session starts with I and then we move from cube to cube till we have used all the tools.'

Vitae's mobile rang again and he reached into his pocket to pick up the phone.

There was a large poster on the wall which had the same crystal cubes on it. Joe walked towards the poster to have a look.

Interrogate

Transcend

Nuptial

Visualise

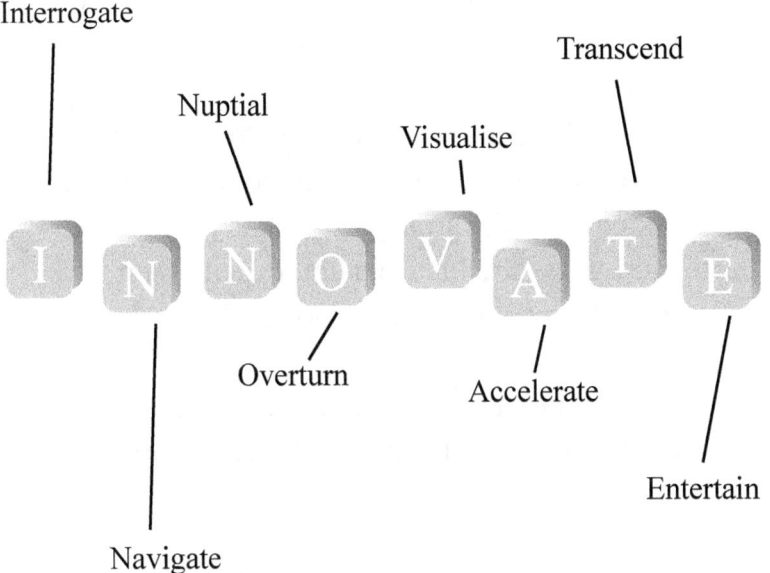

Overturn

Accelerate

Entertain

Navigate

While Joe was looking at the poster, Vitae was having a heated conversation on his mobile. Suddenly he turned to Joe and said, 'I am sorry about this Joe, but I have to leave you now. There's an emergency meeting below.

As I said before, you'll be able to meet all the people who make Eightstorm possible here. I have made all the arrangements for you to meet them. I guess the Interrogation expert is already waiting for you in the next room.'

When Vitae left the cabin, Joe put down the crystal cube on the table and walked towards the door.

He was ready to meet the first Eightstorm expert.

I - Interrogate

'Sit down,' said the red haired man as soon as Joe entered the room. 'So you are here to discover our innovation techniques?' he asked.

'Yes,' said Joe, nodding his head.

'I am the Interrogation expert,' he said, 'I help our team come up with the right questions.'

'Who comes up with the answers?' Joe asked, wondering whether he should have met the person who had all the answers, rather than sitting with this guy who looked like a question-mark.

'All of us. Everyone can get the right answers, once you have the right questions,' the red haired man said. 'Most of the time people are unable to solve problems or find new answers because they don't frame the right question. In fact, some don't even arrive at the question in the first place, so you keep doing the same thing over and over again like the robot arm that screws nuts in the assembly line.'

'Is interrogation an important part of your innovation process?' Joe enquired.

The red haired man looked surprised, 'Of course it is,' he said. 'When confronted with a problem, the first thing any company would try to do is to find a solution. On the other hand an innovative organization would interrogate the problem. It would reframe the problem by asking a smart question about the problem or by defining it in a new way to arrive at a better answer,' the red haired man said with an air of confidence.

'But how do you ask a smart question?' Joe probed.

'That's quite simple,' said the red haired man, 'ask a question for which you have no answer.'

'What was that?' Joe said shaking his head.

'Ask a question for which you have no immediate answer. If you don't have an answer you are forced to find one. That's when you start thinking in new directions and stretching your imagination.'

'In theory it sounds fine,' admitted Joe, 'but is it a practical tool? I mean, how effectively can you use it in the workplace?'

'Let me tell you a small story to illustrate the point,' began the red haired man, 'but before I begin I must warn you, this is just one of the thousand possible ways of using the Interrogation Technique. Don't ever confuse yourself into believing that this is the only way to apply it.'

Joe sat on his chair, listening intently.

'One of our clients is a large telecom operator with millions of telephone subscribers as their primary client base,' the red haired man began. 'They came to us to consult on a specific problem they were facing: Their telephone subscribers weren't paying bills on time. Most of the time consumers put off paying their bills till they had received notices for disconnection. The delayed payments were costing the telecom operator millions of dollars in delayed payments.'

'And how did you manage to find the solution for that?' asked Joe.

'We put it into our Eightstorming session the very next day. And the results were very, very surprising.'

Joe was now all ears as the red haired man spoke. 'Initially we looked at the situation and began asking the routine questions like:

Why don't our customers pay on time?

and

How can we make our customers pay on time?

Then someone in the team asked:

Instead of making the customers pay after using the service, why don't we charge them before they use the service?

Now that was a smart question.

And it was bound to get a smart answer.'

'Well, what was the answer?' enquired Joe.

'No one had asked this question before, so we didn't have an answer right away. But when we put ourselves in this unknown area of thought, we came up with an answer that changed the nature of the Telecom industry.

We came up with the concept of the *prepaid card*.

Instead of waiting for the customer to ring up a huge bill, the telecom operator took an advance payment with this card that would be used long after the customer had purchased it,' the red haired man explained. 'Don't you think that's a real innovation?'

'I think it's quite interesting.' Joe agreed. 'But it makes me feel that companies get innovative only when they're up against a problem. Shouldn't they be coming up with ideas in peace time?'

'Very true,' the red haired man agreed, 'That's why we make it a point to hold Eightstorming sessions every day - problem or no-problem. That way, we ensure the flow of ideas never stop in our organisation.

You see, our number one priority is coming up with innovative ideas that the organisation and our clients can use to keep ourselves ahead of the competition. The only way to do that is teach our people to think creatively and *Interrogation* works really well.'

'You mean, you don't wait for a problem to pop up to solve it,' clarified Joe, 'You do these Eightstorming sessions every day to keep the team sharp.'

'That's right. Like other smart companies, we live on the quality of our ideas,' the red haired man said earnestly, 'and our people have to be on their toes all the time.'

'Last week we were approached by the head of our luxury chain of hotels in Barbados. They had a nice record of customer satisfaction, except for one small hitch. Every customer who came into their hotel for the first time – even those who had pre-booked, had to wait a few minutes for the formalities to be carried out. The guests found this really irritating, especially after a long flight or drive.

The hotel had tried everything to cut short this waiting period, but it really wasn't working. That's when they put up their problem in the Eightstorming session.'

'Did you, once again use the *Interrogation* tool?' Joe asked.

'Yes, we got straight to the point. First we asked the routine questions like: *How can we make the guests wait for shorter periods at your reception?*

Then we moved to smart questions like: *Why do guests hate to wait in your reception?*

Which led to smart answers: *They are stuck there with nothing to do, even if it's for a couple of minutes.*

And this ultimately gave us a seemingly simple, yet powerful solution:

Line up the reception with tall mirrors, so the guests can take a good look at themselves.

While the guests stood watching themselves in the mirror, they'd hardly notice the slight delay and that is precisely how we solved the problem.' the red haired man said.

The Interrogation Technique is all about:

1. Asking a smart question. Move away from the obvious and ask a smart question.

2. How do you know whether you're asking a routine question or a smart one? If you ask a question for which you have no real answer; it's a smart one.

3. When there are no readymade answers, your brain is forced to come up with answers and they'll be smart, because your question is.

4. When you do get to the answer, don't stop at the first one. Let there be a flood of ideas and insights.

*

*Ask a
smart
question*

*If you
want a
smart
solution*

*

'How's it going?,' Vitae asked, popping his head from the half open door. It seemed he was rushing around during his meetings.

'I had an interesting discussion with your Interrogation expert,' Joe said. 'I think it's a fantastic tool that we can use back in our organisation.'

'Of course it is. And so are the other techniques that you'll discover today. Do you want a break, or should I send the next expert on our Eightstorm team to meet you?' Vitae enquired.

'Send him right in,' Joe said with a twinkle in his eye. 'I just can't wait to learn all of your techniques.'

By now a frisky haired man had appeared and Vitae introduced him to Joe.

'Joe, this is Stan, our Navigation expert. Stan meet Joe.'

Saying that Vitae left the room and Joe was left with the frisky haired Stan.

N - Navigate

'I get most of my ideas from movies,' said Stan, the tall man with curly unkept hair, who had worked for an upmarket advertising agency as Creative Director for over twenty years. He was now with Vitae's organisation as the Navigation expert on the Eightstorm team. 'Throughout my ad career, I had to come up with new ideas for advertisements on a daily basis. And a good part of my inspiration came from hollywood flicks. In fact they still do,' the ex-creative director said.

'Do you watch a lot of movies?' Joe asked.

'Yeah. Different kinds. Thrillers, romances, sci-fi. You never know where you'll get your next great idea from.'

'How about the advertising industry itself. Don't you get any inspiration from your own field?' Joe asked.

'If you are looking for gold,' said Stan, 'never dig in your own backyard. You've a much better chance if you go looking elsewhere.'

'You mean, it's better to navigate to fields other than your own, when looking for innovative ideas.' Joe volunteered.

'Absolutely,' said Stan with great enthusiasm. 'Not only do you get fresh perspectives, but even new thought-hooks that can be explored.'

'That's fine,' laughed Stan noticing the bewilderment on Joe's face. 'A thought-hook is nothing but a specific aspect that you take from a foreign field and use it to jumpstart ideas in your own industry.

That means if you are in the banking industry and you're looking at the medical field for inspiration, you will get thought-hooks like allergy tests, crutches, vaccination, antibiotics, shock treatment, blood banks and frozen embryos.

Then you begin to look for parallels in your own industry and explore unexpected resemblances that the comparison brings out.

Take a look at this table here on my laptop.' Stan said.

Medical Thought-Hook :	**Innovative Banking Idea**
Allergy tests :	Using Credit Cards to test credit worthiness of new customers before sanctioning loans
Crutches :	Special accounts with overdraft facility for start-ups
Vaccination :	Built-in insurance with large loans

'It's quite amazing what you can come up with, once you leave the comfort zone of your own industry.'

'Is there any particular industry that you recommend for digging out these idea nuggets?'

'Every field has its own inspiration and importance. I am just giving you examples, but don't limit yourself to any of these industries,' said Stan.

'If I work for a large software development firm, will I be able to navigate to the agricultural field for inspiration?'

'That's an interesting question,' said Stan, reaching for his laptop. 'Let's have a go at that.'

Farming Thought-Hook :	Innovative IT Idea
Rope :	Chat site that hunts for like-minded people and brings them together.
Tractor :	Software that digs out common bugs in the system.
Cow Shed :	Code databank for common use
Fertilizer :	Using unsuccessful programs and turning them into fertilizer for new projects.

'So you see, it's possible to get ideas from any industry as long as you train yourself to look for ideas. Car manufacturers can get inspiration from agriculture, doctors from IT, bricklayers from art, chefs from plumbing... I can go on and on.' said Stan.

'Do you want to try this tool now?'

Joe nodded his head.

'Okay, imagine for a moment that you work for an advertising agency and are responsible for coming up with ideas to promote your client: a furniture outlet. You must navigate to the fishing industry for your inspiration.' Saying that Stan pushed his laptop towards Joe so he could key in his inputs.

<u>Fishing Thought-Hook</u>	:	<u>Innovative Marketing Idea</u>
Baits	:	Hook newly-weds with discount offers on furniture through advertisements.
Fishing Nets	:	Catch people who are buying homes, moving homes or even splitting up their homes through Real Estate agents and sell them your store directly.
Lighthouse	:	Distribute furniture catalogues to flat owners in new buildings.

'That's excellent. You have grasped it quite quickly.' Stan was elated at Joe's attempt.

'The trick is to look at specific aspects in the industry that you are looking at for inspiration and draw out parallels from it for your own industry. Don't get lost in theories. Look at interesting bits and build on it.' Stan added.

'Seems quite interesting. Did you use it a lot during your advertising days?'

'Oh yes,' said Stan. 'I even managed to create an award-winning advertising campaign using *Navigate*. This happened some years ago. The brief had been to create an advertisement for brand X toothpaste. We had to convince consumers that brand X toothpaste was better than its competitors because when used daily, it gave the user, shiny teeth.

If I had looked at the advertising industry itself for inspiration, I'd have seen tv commercials with lots of nice smiling people showing off their shiny teeth. Or I'd have seen people on the beach playing with sea shells and claiming their teeth were just as strong. These, as you know, are the commonly used, cliched advertising visuals which are quite boring. Then I happened to watch a movie about treasure hunters trapped in a dark cave who try to find their way out using glowing diamonds.

It struck me all of a sudden.

If you had extraordinarily bright teeth you could use its glow to find your way in the dark; like navigating through the dark aisle of a movie theater by flashing your teeth. Or hunting for crabs on a dark beach without torches.

That single thought turned into a striking campaign idea for brand X toothpaste.

And it was all because I had navigated to another field for inspiration.' said Stan.

The Navigation Technique is all about:

1. Looking for inspiration in other fields.

2. Focus on specific aspects that can be converted into exciting ideas in your own industry.

*

***Don't dig
for gold
in your own
backyard***

*

Joe was startled by the ringing of his own mobile phone. It was Vitae: 'Joe, I am caught up in a meeting. If you're done with Stan, why don't you get yourself some coffee. I've asked Gosper to meet you next. She will be there in half an hour.'

N - Nuptial

Nuptial, Joe thought, as he sat down waiting for Gosper, his next instructor, *they do have strange names here.*

'Hello,' said Gosper, walking into the room, 'Did I keep you waiting for long?'

'No, I just got here from the café below,' said Joe.

'Nuptial sounds like a strange name, doesn't it for a creative thinking tool?' Gosper asked. 'Literally *Nuptial* indicates marriage, and this technique is all about combining two elements to form a third. It is like taking two existing concepts and bringing it together to give you an offspring which is new, different and much more advanced than its parents.'

'Sounds interesting,' said Joe.

'Do you know from where Gutenberg got the idea of the printing press?' Gosper asked.

'No,' said Joe.

'From a wine press,' explained Gosper. 'He took the idea of a wine press and mixed it with a coin punch. Bingo! the letter press was born.

Someone got the idea of making a portable device that can play mp3 songs and we got our iPod.

They put a camera into our mobile phones and we got the camera phone.

Computers are convenient but bulky machines. Books are handy sources of information but limited by their physical size. Someone mixed them up and we got the notebook.

Kids love to eat chocolates. Kids also love to play with toys. But what if you put a toy inside the chocolate? You get a Kinder Surprise.

So you see, the nuptial technique is all about combining existing concepts to get a new idea,' said Gosper.

'This sounds great, but when using the Nuptial technique how does one go about selecting the elements to combine?' asked Joe.

'That depends upon your requirement,' Gosper explained. 'If you are in the banking industry and trying to come up with a new kind of credit card, why not mix a movie theater with a restaurant and come up with a card that gives you points every time you go to the movies towards a free dinner.

Or imagine you are in the IT industry and creating PCs for the blind. You could combine braille keyboards with sound-emitting mouses and create a new PC for the visually challenged.'

'That's nice,' said Joe. 'I guess it's even possible to come up with non-commercial ideas using this technique.'

'Of course it is,' said Gosper. 'It all depends upon your ability to combine and the amount of informative elements that you are carrying. The more information that you have, the more your chances of making unexpected combinations and sparking off a really great idea.

This is also the reason why some of the most creative people in human history have also been the most curious. They were hungry for new information and kept on gathering it for no apparent reason.

And then one fine day – BANG! – the elements combine in a striking manner and a groundbreaking idea is born.'

The Nuptial Technique is all about:

1. Merging diverse elements to get a new idea.

2. Be open to information that can serve as the raw material for new combinations.

*

*Merge one concept
with another*

And you have a new idea.

*

What's Vitae up to now, thought Joe as he sat down and opened his laptop. *I guess, I better take note of these points before I forget it.* He opened a fresh document in his laptop and began keying in his thoughts:

Interrogate: Ask a smart question.
How can I use it at my company?

Navigate: Seek inspiration from other fields.
Can we take a look at scuba diving for inspiration.

Nuptial: Combine diverse elements and get a new idea.
Must think about this one.

As he sat typing on his laptop, he could hear footsteps in the corridor. *Must be the next Eightstormer,* Joe thought. *Let's see what this person has got to offer.*

O - Overturn

Joe looked up when Mag entered.

'Hi' said Joe, getting up to shake hands with her. 'Do you mind if I finish these notes?'

'No, it's fine.'

'I've already met three of the Eightstorm experts here,' Joe said without looking up from him laptop. 'You have an interesting team here.'

'We sure do. You should see the fun we have

during our Eightstorming sessions. For many companies brainstorming is a horrid affair. Here we enjoy our sessions. I guess it is because of the tools that we are using,' Mag explained. 'Vitae must already have told you about my role in these sessions. I am the Overturn expert.'

'Sounds interesting,' said Joe.

'It is, especially when you have tried the other tools during a creative thinking session and want something even more different.'

'So what is Overturn?' Joe asked closing his laptop.

'It's all about thinking in opposites,' Mag explained. 'Most of the time we tend to think straight. If we've got a straight problem, we try to get a straight answer. But you have a better chance of getting an answer, if you go in the opposite direction.'

Joe smiled. What Mag said made perfect sense

to him. He remembered a drawing competition he had entered a long time ago when he was a kid and still in school. The instructor had asked the kids to draw a poster to show their support to the environment. Everyone drew trees and grass and ponds. He was the only one who drew an upside down tree and wrote beneath it: *Don't turn the world upside down for us.*

He won the first prize.

'Although it sounds like a fairly simple technique,' Mag continued, 'most people say it is a tough tool to use, especially in the beginning. I guess, we are so used to thinking straight, it is really tough to take a 180-degree look at things.'

'Very true.' Joe agreed. 'We are all caught up in thinking straight most of the time, it's a bit too much to change direction.'

'This is exactly what happed at a livestock company under the Group,' Mag said turning the temperature down on the AC control. 'The Head of Operations approached us with a very strange problem. You see, they breed livestock which goes to a large Abattoir where the livestock is butchered and gets packed for distribution to supermarkets and retail outlets.

The difficulty was at the Abattoir. The cattle were transported from the farm to a pen in the Abattoir from where they were led to the butchery. Since animals can sense danger without really seeing anything, they refused to enter the trap door that led to the butchery. It took a lot of time and effort to round them up and take them to the butchery. They tried a lot of things, but nothing worked. That's when the Head of Operations posted his problem for Eightstorming.'

'So anyone in your organisation can put up these kinds of requests?' Joe asked, opening up his laptop again, getting ready to take down notes.

'Sure, since we have a trained team on board,

we put it straight into our next session.' Mag clarified.

'And were you able to look at the situation in the Abattoir in a new way,' Joe inquired.

'Yes, the opposite way,' Mag said with a smile. 'We overturned their problem. Instead of trying to bring the cattle to the butchery, we tried to prevent them from entering the butchery. As I told you before, the pen is separated from the butchery by a trap door. By making the pen smaller we crowded up the place and the cattle made a stampede towards the trap door that led them to the butchery.'

Nice idea, but what a revolting example, thought Joe as he hit the keys on his laptop.

Beep. It was his mobile with another *Sorry I'm held up* message from Vitae. The only highlight of the sms was that his next instructor was waiting for him in the room at the end of the corridor.

The Overturn Technique is all about:

1. Looking at the situation in the opposite way.

2. Taking a u-turn while everyone goes straight, will lead to pleasant surprises when you are on the creative highway.

*

***When
the whole
world zigs***

Zag

*

V - Visualise

Everything about the next room was colourful. Large boastful posters covered the walls. They were nicely complimented by bright orange coloured tables and chairs. Joe pulled up one of the bright chairs and sat down waiting for the next Eightstormer to come in.

'Oh! you are already here,' said Mackenzie as he entered the room. 'I am quite sure you have an idea about how our company works, by now.' he said taking his seat.

'Now it's time to discover the power of visualisation,' Mackenzie continued. 'The first thing that we need to realise is that most of us tend to think and communicate in words. Just look at the amount of internal emails that we receive and send.'

'That's true,' said Joe, 'and considering that words are the easiest way to communicate, it's not surprising.'

'When you are trying to do things beyond the ordinary, you need a system that can break the everyday convenience factor. That's why you need to think in visuals instead of words.

Look at these sketches here,' said Mackenzie.

'Imagine that your company is fishing for new clients and unable to do so. A simple scribble like this could put everything into perspective.' Mackenzie waved his black marker as he spoke. 'You realise in an instant that you are looking in the wrong place for new clients and the obvious answer is to charter a new course of action.'

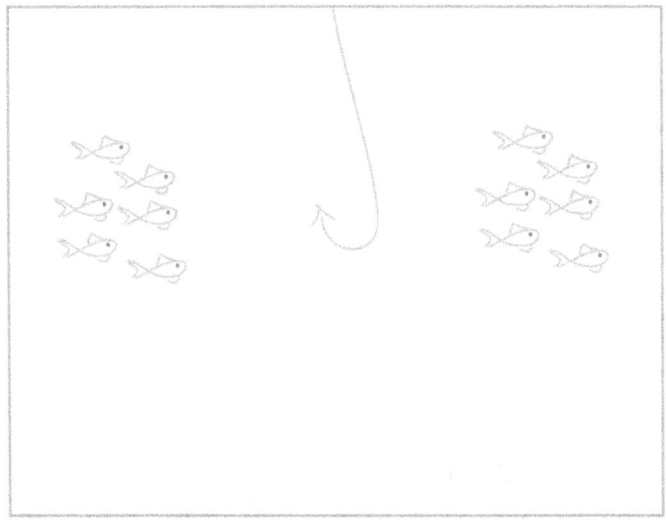

'I can see that your visualising technique can define a problem. But can you solve it?' Joe asked.

'The solution lies in a scribble like this,' said Mackenzie.

'What's this, a multiple bait?'

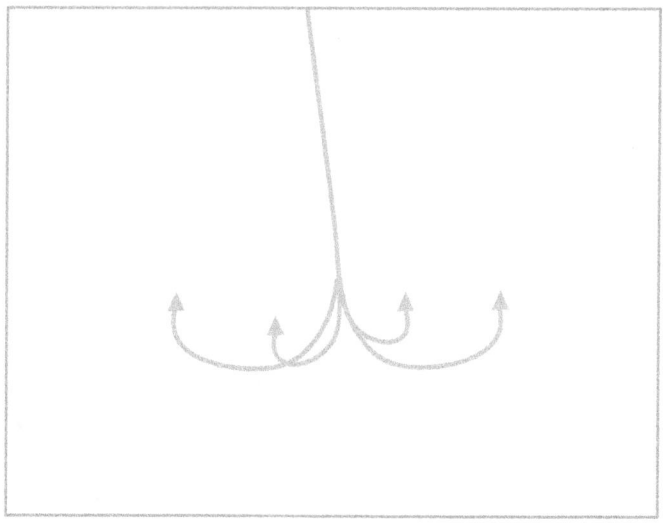

'Yes,' said Mackenzie. 'This is the initial solution to your problem - multiple baits. It means you have a better chance of catching clients if you have more people on your team. So you need to recruit more sales staff to give you better results. Now let's look at the second solution for the same problem.'

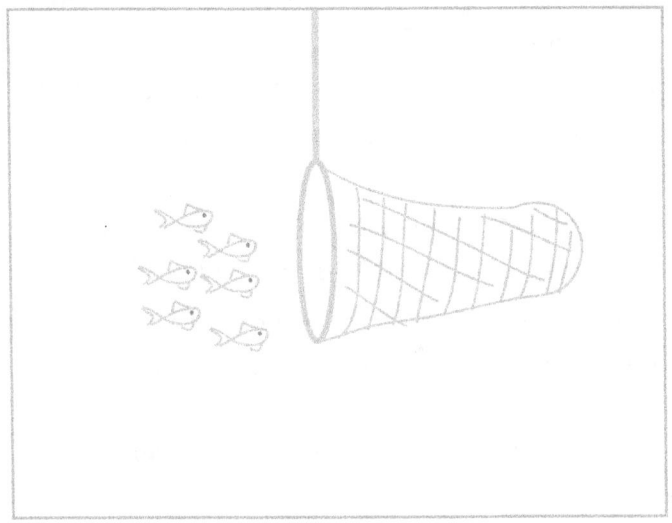

'While with the bait you were trying to hook individual clients, the fishing net lets you catch a lot of clients at once. You just need to be at a place where your prospective clients are found in large numbers, like an exhibition or conference.

Once you are in the midst of your prospects, make yourself irresistible with an exciting offer that attracts them to your net.'

'It all sounds very simple,' Joe said. 'But at the same time it makes sense. Often we are too close to our business in our day-to-day life and we miss the big picture. I guess the visual technique puts everything into perspective, neatly.'

'The beauty about the visual technique is that you can keep on scribbling solutions like these till you have a substantial number of ideas that you can try out.' Mackenzie explained.

'Fine,' said Joe nodding in agreement. 'Can we look at some more examples?'

'Sure,' said Mackenzie, reaching out for his scribbling pad.

'Does this visual make any sense?' Mackenzie asked.

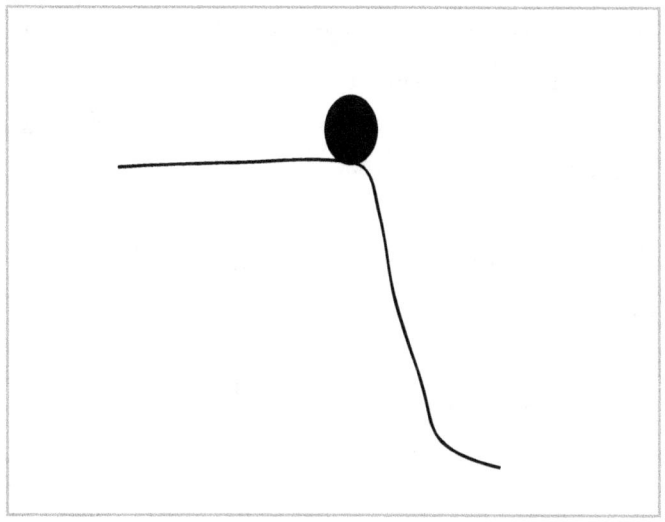

'A precariously poised boulder?'

Mackenzie smiled. 'This is the visual that we drew when we were analysing the position of the media company within our group. They were operating with a single, large client. In effect they were the boulder on the ledge.'

'Did the visual make them uneasy?'

'Oh yes, it did. It made all of us nervous. The

head of media hadn't realised the danger that they were sitting on. The thought of that sole client cutting short their contract, made us shudder!'

'So what did you do about the situation?' Joe wanted to know.

'Well, we drew another scribble.'

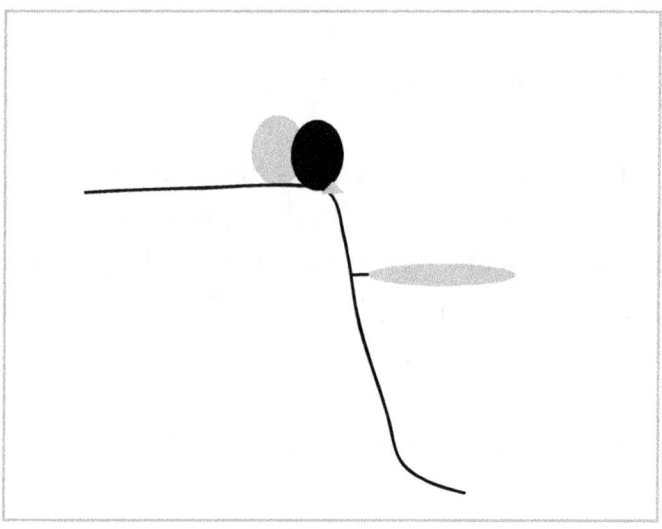

'Three options popped up with this scribble.' Mackenzie explained.

'We could find a second client who would help us survive even if the first client had quit.

Secondly, we could provide attentive service to our existing client and ensure that they wouldn't budge.

And thirdly we could build a safety net for the company by diversifying into other media businesses.

Simple but effective, isn't it! That's the beauty of the visual technique.' Mackenzie was now scribbling a caption on his notepad as he spoke.

The Visual Technique is all about:

1. Visualising the problem

2. Visualising the solution

*

*Think
in
Visuals*

*

Joe left the room whistling. He was in high spirits. The scribbling had suddenly opened his mind to new possibilities at his own office. For once that day, he wasn't worried that Vitae was dashing from meeting to meeting without seeing him. He decided to check out who was next on the list with the receptionist in the main building. Vitae had been smart enough to schedule the rest of the team in quick succession for him in the conference room.

There we go, thought Joe, *three more experts and I am an Eightstormer myself.*

A - Accelerate

The moment Joe entered the conference room, he was handed a clean sheet of A4 paper by a nervous looking chap.

'Hi, I am Martin. You can have this paper, Mr. Joe.'

Is this man rushed for time or is he accelerating things, wondered Joe as he took his seat.

Before we start this session,' warned Martin, 'I

want you to write down 10 ideas on how to save a kid trapped in a burning house. And I need it in the next 2 minutes. Here is your paper and pen and your time starts now.'

Joe was unsettled by the sudden request, but was beginning to like the queer habits of this organisation, and so he took the pen and began writing furiously:

1. Call 999 and help them locate the house to save the kid.

2. Use the fire extinguisher to put out the fire and then enter the house.

3. If there are no fire extinguishers, use water or sand to control the flames.

4. Shout for help, so passers-by can come and help.

5. Go around the house to find alternative ways to get in.

6. Use a ladder to get to the upper floor and search for the kid.

7. Get hold of the door mats. Wrap it around you for protection against the flames and run inside.

8. If there are trees around, break off the branches and use it to beat down the flames as you get in.

9. Look for the lawn sprinkler. Yank off the top and use it as a water hose to douse the flames.

10. Throw a rope for the kid if he's standing on the balcony and yank the rope suddenly. Catch the kid as he falls down.

'That's pretty good. You did it in five minutes. That's three minutes over the allotted time, but for a first-timer, that's okay,' said Martin, looking at the beaming Joe.

'I didn't know I could think so fast.'

'Most people I train have the same problem. They don't realise how quickly they can generate ideas, especially in such a short time. Throughout our life, we have been taught that thinking is a long drawn out process. While in college and later on in our work places we were expected to find solutions after days and weeks of thinking. Even the conventional brainstorming session that you come across is a grilling session of endless hours of discussion to get that breakthrough idea.

What we don't realise is that the human brain is a wonderful instrument. Give it a problem and give it two minutes to give you ten answers. And you'll get twelve answers that are so good, you'll wonder where it came from.'

'Does it happen all the time?' questioned Joe.

'Every time without fail. In my ten years in this company, I have seen it happening again and again.

The best part of the Acceleration technique is that it gets rid of two thinking problems at the same time.

The *problem of the big answer* and the *fear of innovation*.

Let's look at the *big answer* problem first. When you are looking out for a new idea or a new solution for a problem, you are looking for the one big idea that can solve it all. That single big idea doesn't come out easily. Instead what you can get quickly are small bright ideas that can light up your path to the altar of the big idea. This is what our Acceleration Technique provides. Lots of small ideas that will switch your creative thinking into a higher gear.

Now, let's examine the *fear of innovation*. Most of us have never been taught to use the creative prowess of our amazing brain or realised that creative thinking is easier than we imagine, and so the moment we have this extraordinary task of coming up with ideas, we feel paralyzed. There's nothing like the Acceleration technique to crank up your brain and get the ideas flowing,' Martin explained.

The Acceleration Technique is all about:

1. Thinking in bursts.

2. Jot down your thoughts as fast as it emerges. This prevents you from judging your own ideas.

*

Ideate fast

*Because
the best
thoughts
come out
before you
judge*

*

T - Transcend

This is getting even more interesting Joe thought as Martin left the conference room. *Let's see what the next one is all about.*

'I can see that you are quite overwhelmed with our methods,' Wal said entering the room. 'Most of the people who go through this take a week's time to take it all in.'

'It's been a whirlwind learning experience.' Joe admitted.

'Of all the tools that you have come across here,' Wal said, 'Transcend is the one that you will find difficult to master. But if you do that, I guarantee you, the results will be amazing.'

'The sessions here have been interesting, one after the other. What makes the Transcend tool so special,' Joe enquired.

'The Transcend Technique is all about going beyond the obvious. But the problem with the obvious is that it isn't so obvious.' Wal explained.

'Why isn't the obvious so obvious?' Joe asked innocently.

'Imagine you are sitting in a brainstorming session and trying to cough up ideas,' Wal said. 'If you aren't trained, you might not realise that the initial ideas which pop-up would most probably be rehashed ideas. These could in reality be concepts that you might have heard or seen somewhere, which are now popping up under the pressure of the situation and are looking like original thoughts.

You might have seen people getting all worked up during meetings, suddenly declaring - *I've got an amazing idea!*

Chances are, they've suddenly discovered an idea, which is just an obvious thought looking like a fresh one.

The Transcend technique reminds you that most of the thoughts that we get initially in any brainstorming session would be second-hand thoughts.

Recognising the obvious is step number one.

Step two is transcending the obvious.' Wal explained.

'How do you differentiate the obvious from an original thought?' Joe inquired.

'That's a tough question,' Wal admitted, 'There are no hard and fast rules to do that. What may look original to you, may in reality be an obvious idea. It's a gut decision you make, something you develop over the years.'

'So, how do you move with a technique that has no clear boundaries?' Joe asked.

'The Transcend technique assumes that all the ideas that you get in the first 15 minutes of your brainstorming session are obvious ones,' Wal explained. 'Then it asks you to leap.'

'Leap?' Joe asked surprised.

'Yeah. Leap over the obvious.' Wal said.

'Have you ever been able to do that?' Joe wanted to know.

'Of course. Why not? Every tool that we're discussing here has got a practical application. Do you think we'd talk about something that we cannot use?' Wal asked.

'What I meant was, can you give me an example of this technique in use?'

'Yeah, I was coming to that part.' Wal replied. 'The IT guys in our Group were looking for ways to stop personal use of the net. They did a dipstick survey and found that 60% of our employees spent more time on the net for personal reasons than on work-related issues. They wanted to reduce this time wastage without raising a hue and cry about it. In fact they tried a couple of things on their own, but then they thought it would be better to let the Eightstorming team to take care of it.'

'I am sure you must have discussed lots of obvious ways to end the private usage,' Joe volunteered.

'Yes, the Eightstorming session did start off with suggestions like using cctvs to monitor staff and disabling chat applications from our computers. But then we realised that most of these ideas were impractical.

Then someone in the team came up with a suggestion of installing a bogus application called Performance Monitor on everyone's desktop. The new application had a roving eye as its icon and it couldn't be uninstalled. Suddenly everyone felt like they were being watched. As it was a desktop performance-monitoring software, no one could question the software's intention.

Till that suggestion came along we were on the obvious track, but suddenly we had risen over the mundane and transcended to a new plane.' Wal said.

'Was the idea successful? I mean, did the personal use of net come down?' Joe wanted to know.

'Come down?' Wal's voice was triumphant. 'It almost vanished overnight.'

The Transcend Technique is all about:

1. Recognising that most of the initial ideas generated during a discussion would be obvious ones.

2. The trick is to recognise the weakness of these ideas and use it as a base from where you can leap.

*

**_Surround
yourself
with obvious
ideas._**

Then leap over it

*

E - Entertain

Wal's session ended when Alan walked in. 'Hi, you must be Joe, the chap who's out to learn our little secret. I am Alan. I shall be taking you through *Entertain*, the last tool in the Eightstorming process.'

'*Entertain* sounds fun, doesn't it!'

'Yes, it's a fun technique. Tell me one thing, do you crack a lot of jokes in your company?' Alan asked.

'Jokes? No, we're too busy for that,' Joe said

without really thinking. The look on Alan's face made him realise that he'd said something wrong.

'That means you're too busy to get innovative and you're missing a chance to be at your creative best.' Alan shot back.

'*Entertain* is all about opening up your mind to unexpected creative accidents. Here in our office, if we are looking for new ideas, or if we are stuck with a problem, we create a few jokes around the subject. Most of the time it would be something silly or illogical. The whole team horses around the topic and one thing leads to another and before we know it, something new pops out.' Alan explained.

'I have read somewhere that all jokes have one thing in common: They have an unexpected twist,' Joe put in. 'Maybe it's the same unexpected twist that's triggering off those new ideas.'

'Could be, but what we need to remember is to keep our objectives in sight during these discussions,' Alan continued. 'If for example you're discussing the problem of late-comers in your office, you better play around with that specific topic. Or you'll end up with a lot of gags with no specific direction. Someone in the team should always be looking out for those nuggets of gold in the midst of all that fun.'

'Did you really have an entertainment session to solve the problem of late-comers?' Joe enquired.

'Oh yes, we did once.' Alan explained. 'And it was during that session someone came up with a funny idea of having a "Champion Late Comer Award" for the office. The idea was to paste photos on the notice-board and let everyone vote for the winner. The entire office was allowed to participate in the game and people started turning up early with their camera-phones to catch the unfortunate winner. The real late-comers started coming in early to avoid the harassment. In short, the problem was solved without installing any monitoring equipment or issuing memos.'

'I can see that it's a new way to solve problems, but when you are looking for innovative ideas, do you think this kind of entertainment will yield results?' Joe said doubtfully.

Alan smiled. 'Have you heard of the company that planned to chop off the legs of its employees to stop them from running away from the company and joining a competitor?'

'That's not true. Is it?' Joe asked, 'No company would dare to do that.'

'This particular company would,' Alan said, 'they had spent a lot of time and effort to train their new recruits. But as soon as the staff were trained, a competing firm offered the new staff higher pay and lured them away. The company which was losing its people was so frustrated that one HR manager in the company suggested they chop off the legs of those traitor employees.'

'He must have been joking,' Joe said.

'Of course, he was. But guess what the joke led to! An entire program to recruit and train handicapped people. Plus a workplace which was thoughtfully revamped to accommodate people with special needs, like specially fitted out toilets, ramps for wheelchairs on doorways and lots of other benefits. All these changes made it simply impossible for new recruits to move out once their training was over.'

'That's absolutely amazing,' gasped Joe.

'That's the power of the Entertainment tool. When you joke, you throw up unexpected combinations of thoughts that can turn your discussion into a hotbed of ideas. Here in our company when someone starts fooling around a subject, we know we are going to strike gold any moment.' Alan explained.

The Entertainment Technique is all about:

1. Using humour to open your mind to new ideas.

2. Then bringing in logic to connect these seemingly illogical points to get a completely new solution for your problem.

*

*Laugh
your way
to an
idea*

*

Joe sat down with a cup of coffee trying to recollect everything that he had learned in one extraordinary day. There was no sign of Vitae yet but somehow he felt relaxed.

He realised in an instant what had gone wrong in his own company. The mistake that had led his President to commit suicide seemed so apparent now. He wondered how many companies that ignore innovation would face the same peril.

A company without a bank of ideas could go bankrupt any day, he typed into his laptop.

Joe realised that the time had come for him to find the answers that would save his company. He had learned a powerful process and now it was time to use it.

What if I applied the Interrogation Technique in my company he typed.

A few moments later the answers began to appear. Startling answers. Not only from the

Interrogation Technique. But from Navigate and Nuptial and Overturn. He tried to Visualise and the result was a diagram that gave a new look to the problem that he faced back home. He tried Acceleration and got ten unique answers in two minutes. Even Entertain gave him more solutions than he had anticipated.

Now Joe was swamped with ideas and concepts. He had more than he wanted to save his precariously poised organisation. He was ready to reap the rewards of Eightstorm. It was time to fly back home on the wings of innovation.

The last thing he did before leaving Vitae's office was shoot off a message to Vitae: *Thanks buddy. Thanks for everything.*

Using INNOVATE

There are certain rules to be followed while Eightstorming in your workplace.

1. Sessions should always be conducted by someone who has practiced using all the 8 tools.

2. Use each tool separately. Mixing up tools will muddle up your session.

3. Start with Interrogate. Give the participants a couple of minutes to get tuned to the technique. Give a few examples of the Interrogation tool in action.

4. Assign a non-participating person to jot down all the ideas that are generated - however silly or idiotic they may sound.

5. Move on to the second tool only when the

first tool has been satisfactorily exploited.

6. Use lots of examples to illustrate the use of each tool.

7. Keep the negative thinkers, idea killers and cynics out of the session. It will lead to more productive and smoother sessions.

8. Always start with a clear plan of action and keep track of your achievements.

9. Have a second session to sort the ideas generated.

10. Upload the selected ideas into a common folder that everyone in the company has access to. Have a separate section for non-selected ideas.

Eightstorming Session
Sample Sheet

1. We are meeting to discuss:

2. How can we interrogate this situation:

3. Let's navigate to another field. List down 5 common aspects from that field and find connections to our situation:

4. How can we combine two diverse elements that will give us a new take on our current situation:

5. Can we overturn the situation and look at it from the opposite direction:

6. If we sketch the situation and the solution, what will emerge:

7. Jot down 10 ideas to make this situation better in the next 2 minutes:

8. List down the obvious solutions to our current problem. Now transcend it:

9. What funny thoughts can we associate with this situation:

Ideas Generated:_____

_____

_____

_____

Future Course of Action:

_____

_____

Will your company INNOVATE or Perish?

This is a question that only you can answer. But like Vitae and his friend Joe, I have seen it work again and again. In ad agencies, banks, software development companies... the list really goes on.

In fact, it doesn't matter which industry you are in. As long as you take the time and effort to practice the eight tools, Eightstorm is bound to give you all the firepower you need to come up with innovative solutions. Trust me.

Acknowledgements

Over the years, I have been influenced by several colleagues, clients and friends. My thanks to all.

I also express my gratitude to my parents **Dharmarajan** and **Thankamani**, my wife **Suvarna** and my son **Ojus**.

About the Author

Kishore Dharmarajan wrote copy for several international advertising agencies including M&C Saatchi, before forming Eureka Advertising, a creative boutique offering innovative branding and marketing solutions for high profile clients in Dubai, United Arab Emirates.

Kishore conducts Eightstorm seminars for businesses bent on turning its people into powerful innovators and can be contacted by email: kishoreed@gmail.com or online at www.eightstorm.com.

www.ingramcontent.com/pod-product-compliance
Lightning Source LLC
Chambersburg PA
CBHW071225170526
45165CB00003B/989